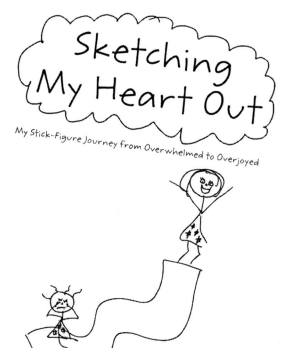

Sketching My Heart Out

My Stick-Figure Journey from Overwhelmed to Overjoyed

Susie Longfellow   •   Foreword by Melody Carlson

Pleasant Word
A Division of WinePress Group
PW

Pleasant Word (a division of WinePress Publishing, PO Box 428, Enumclaw, WA 98022) functions only as book publisher. As such, the ultimate design, content, editorial accuracy, and views expressed or implied in this work are those of the author.

ISBN 13: 978-1-4141-0672-4
ISBN 10: 1-4141-0672-6
Library of Congress Catalog Card Number: 2008911410

Dedicated to three of my biggest
blessings from God

Jennifer
Jonathan
Carolyn

Foreword

I FIRST READ *Sketching My Heart Out* years ago when it was still in the form of some slightly rough-looking three-by-five cards. But the honest transparency of Susie Longfellow's story, told through childlike illustrations and scripture, was truly moving. And it remains memorable today.

And yet at that time (having worked in publishing and written a few books) I had no idea how to make those quirky little cards into a book that could sit on a bookshelf and be accessible to readers. I was truly perplexed. Well, here it is now—no longer a handful of dog-eared cards for one or two people to experience but *a real book* to touch many. A simple little book with some really big truths.

Because no matter who you are, life never goes smoothly, easily, perfectly—not for very long anyway. Oh, we can all be fooled into thinking that's how it's supposed to be, but sooner or later everyone is hit with challenges, disappointments, heartaches…. And yet Susie bravely embraces these hard times with truth, humor, and hope.

No, this isn't a book that will win the Pulitzer (although you never know) but it does offer the kind of encouragement that Jesus must've been talking about when he told us to become like children. And being childlike in that way means humbling ourselves, trusting God in the thick of trouble, and taking his promises to heart. This book does just that. Way to go, Susie!

> *I tell you the truth, unless you change and become like little children, you will never enter the kingdom of heaven. Therefore, whoever humbles himself like this child is the greatest in the kingdom of heaven.*
>
> —Matthew 18:3-4

Melody Carlson, author of many books for women, teens, and children

Introduction

THIS BOOK STARTED in my laundry basket. At forty-five, I viewed my life as a disaster. I believed in God, but I believed I was in control—talk about a hopeless feeling! My church background had taught me rules and consequences, and I got some good from it for sure, but I had missed the main point of the Bible. I didn't understand what my relationship with Christ could be like. I even thought I had to have a middleman to do my talking!

I believed God didn't like me and had given up on me. In excruciating pain and feeling so scared, I didn't have the energy to read any book that might help. But I did write Philippians 4:6–7 on a three-by-five-inch card, sit in my laundry basket (the only private place I had), cry, and read that card again and again:

> In nothing be anxious, but in everything, by prayer and petition with thanksgiving, let your requests be made known to God. And the peace of God, which surpasses all understanding, will guard your hearts and your thoughts in Christ Jesus.
>
> —WEB

I sank deeper into the laundry, but as that three-by-five card became tattered and torn, I started to become bright and shiny.

That one three-by-five card grew to many cards. I started drawing (I use the term loosely) stick figures of me conversing with God, the drawings on the cards reflecting how I felt. I argued with God, misunderstood, and then finally got it—or so I thought. My lessons from God were like my lessons with a golf pro. At my first lesson the pro told me two things I needed to do to improve my game. I was ecstatic. "I'm only doing two things wrong!" I said. "No, that's all you can handle right now," the pro answered. Thankfully, that's just how God teaches us.

I moved from laundry-basket tears to joy and laughter. My journey in life took a different path. I had been doing a lot that was unhealthy for me. I started seeing life differently. I saw my place in life differently. I even saw a reason for my being here!

I'd like to say the journey was short and easy and that I learned quickly. That would be a lie. (And it's not nice to lie in Christian books, or in any book or anywhere, for that matter.) I moved forward, slipped, tripped, and just plain blew it many, many times.

The reason I can share these personal thoughts now is because I know I'm not the only one who's ever tried to be God. If you are thinking that you have better plans than God, I highly recommend letting go of that thought! Following the path God shows you is such a peaceful, loving, exciting way through life. I know because I have tried life both ways.

I'm not a neat package, but I am full of passion. That's what I want my "rustic" art and less-than-perfect penmanship to communicate. My mom used to tell me it was OK to color outside the lines; what do you think God would say about my style? God sees the heart. I like to think he would enjoy the story of my journey to him, and I hope you do too.

"For my thoughts are not your thoughts,
neither are your ways my ways,"
declares the LORD.

Isaiah 55:8

Rest in the LORD and wait
patiently for Him;

Psalm 37:7 (NASB)

Draw near to God,
and
he will draw near to you.

James 4:8 (WEB)

I am

I feel like God
is talking directly
to me.

Anxiety in a man's
heart weighs it down,
but a kind word makes it glad.

Proverbs 12:25 (WEB)

That's why we can be so sure that
every detail in our lives of love for
God is worked into something good.

Romans 8:28 (MESSAGE)

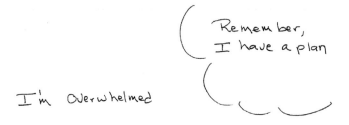

I'm Overwhelmed

In nothing be anxious, but in everything,
by prayer and petition with thanksgiving,
let your requests be made known to God.
And the peace of God, which surpasses
all understanding, will guard your
hearts and your thoughts in Christ Jesus.

Philippians 4:6–7 (WEB)

What a God! His road stretches straight and smooth.
Every GOD-direction is road-tested.
Everyone who runs toward him makes it.

Psalm 18:30 (MESSAGE)

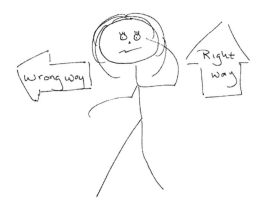

Cast all your anxiety on him because
he cares for you.

1 Peter 5:7

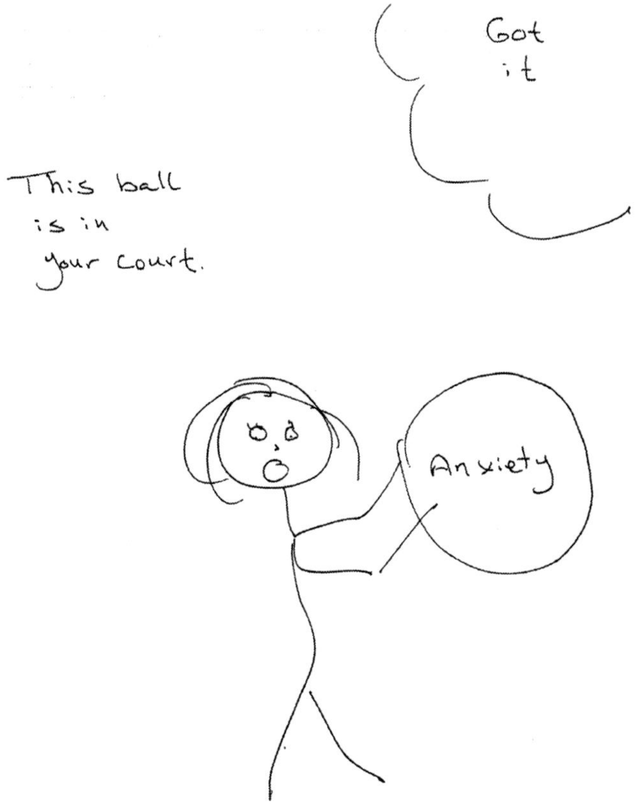
Got it
This ball is in your court.
Anxiety

Come to me, all you who labor and are heavily
burdened, and I will give you rest.

Matthew 11:28 (WEB)

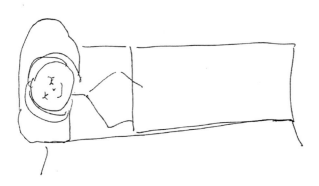

Therefore I tell you, don't be anxious for your life:
what you will eat, or what you will drink;
nor yet for your body, what you will wear.
Isn't life more than food,
and the body more than clothing?

Matthew 6:25 (WEB)

"Behold, I am the LORD,
the God of all flesh;
is anything too difficult for Me?"

Jeremiah 32:27 (NASB)

Always,
I made you,
I love you

God can handle the
whole world and still
have time for me.

Do not fear, for I am with you;
Do not anxiously look about you,
for I am your God I will strengthen you,
surely I will help you,
Surely I will uphold you
with My righteous right hand.

Isaiah 41:10 (NASB)

A wise man will hear and increase in learning,
And a man of understanding
will acquire wise counsel.

Proverbs 1:5 (NASB)

"For I know the plans I have for you,"
declares the LORD, "plans to prosper you
and not to harm you, plans to give
you hope and a future."

Jeremiah 29:11

If the LORD delights in a man's way,
he makes his steps firm; though he stumble,
he will not fall, for the LORD upholds
him with his hand.

Psalm 37:23–24

Funny, when I look up
I stumble less
than when I look down.

Do not be afraid of sudden fear Nor of the onslaught
of the wicked when it comes; For the LORD
will be your confidence And will keep your
foot from being caught.

Proverbs 3:25–26 (NASB)

Always

Caught me again

Direct me in the path of your commandments,
for I delight in them.

Psalm 119:35 (WEB)

I like
walking together

Sure beats
my ole path.

Look at this: look who got picked by God!
He listens the split second I call to him.

Psalm 4:3 (MESSAGE)

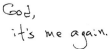

Every Scripture is God-breathed and profitable
for teaching, for reproof, for correction,
and for instruction in righteousness.

2 Timothy 3:16 (WEB)

I do have all the answers

Once again the answer is in here.

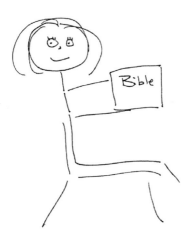

Figure out what will please Christ,
and then do it.

Ephesians 5:10 (MESSAGE)

You've come to
the right place

I want to know
you better, know what
makes you happy.

I will instruct you and teach you in the way
which you shall go. I will counsel
you with my eye on you.

Psalm 32:8 (WEB)

Watch over your heart with all diligence,
For from it flow the springs of life.

Proverbs 4:23 (NASB)

nice
work

Read

Bible

Sermon

Bible

Fellowship

Bible

For if you forgive men their trespasses,
your heavenly Father will also forgive you.

Matthew 6:14 (WEB)

I'll be the judge
Keep trying
I can say I forgive,
but I don't feel it.
ouch
it hurts

I'm telling you to love your enemies.
Let them bring out the best in you,
not the worst. When someone gives
you a hard time, respond with the
energies of prayer, for then you are
working out of your true selves,
your God-created selves.

Matthew 5:44, (MESSAGE)

I appreciate your obedience. Your heart is softening as you pray

I'm praying you will soften my heart. I'm trying but this isn't natural.

Wisdom is before the face of one who has
understanding.

Proverbs 17:24 (WEB)

Wise
Observation

Amazing, the answer
is always here.

No temptation has taken you except what is
common to man. God is faithful, who will not
allow you to be tempted above what you are able,
but will with the temptation also make the way of
escape, that you may be able to endure it.

1 Corinthians 10:13 (WEB)

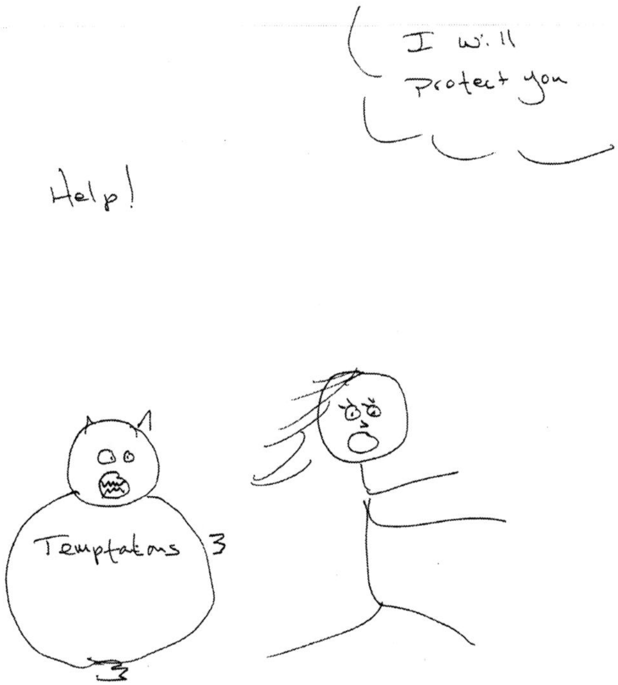
I will protect you
Help!
Temptations

Therefore whatever you desire for men
to do to you, you shall also do to them;
for this is the law and the prophets.

Matthew 7:12 (WEB)

Woe to the one who quarrels with his Maker.

Isaiah 45:9 (NASB)

I know
you aren't
thinking right

I think you're wrong,
I'm worthless.

Charm can mislead and beauty soon fades.
The woman to be admired and praised is the
woman who lives in the Fear-of-GOD.

Proverbs 31:30 (MESSAGE)

This is
true beauty

you are
beautiful

← growing heart

In all your ways acknowledge him,
and he will make your paths straight.

Proverbs 3:6 (WEB)

I like
to hear that

I love you, God.
Please guide me

Therefore, since we are surrounded by such a great
cloud of witnesses, let us throw off everything that
hinders and the sin that so easily entangles,
and let us run with perseverance
the race marked out for us.

Hebrews 12:1

Peace I leave with you. My peace I give to you;
not as the world gives, give I to you.
Don't let your heart be troubled,
neither let it be fearful.

John 14:27 (WEB)

Even so, let your light shine before men;
that they may see your good works,
and glorify your Father who is in heaven.

Matthew 5:16 (WEB)

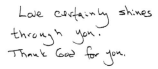

Whether therefore you eat, or drink,
or whatever you do,
do all to the glory of God.

1 Corinthians 10:31 (WEB)

This job
is a bummer

But don't forget to be doing good and sharing,
for with such sacrifices God is well pleased.

Hebrews 13:16 (WEB)

Listen carefully to my wisdom;
take to heart what
I can teach you.

Proverbs 22:17 (MESSAGE)

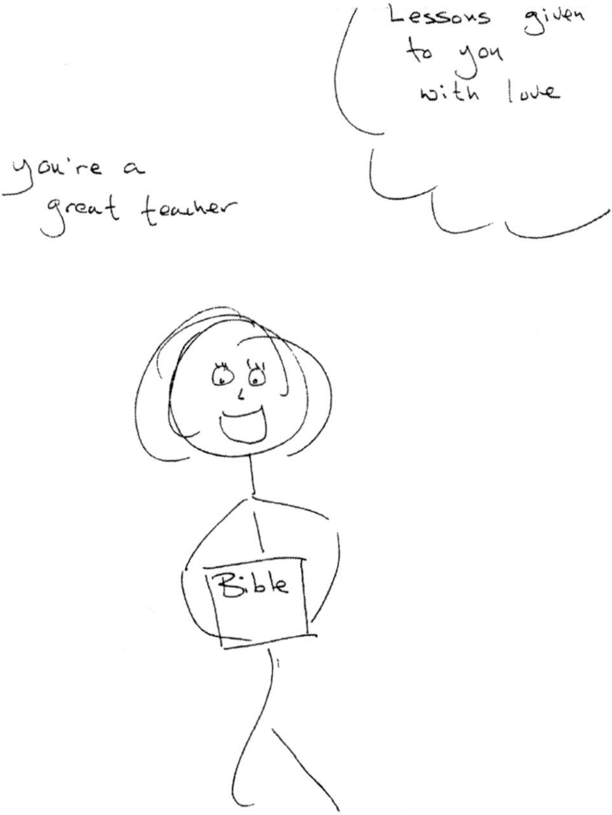
Lessons given
to you
with love
you're a
great teacher
Bible

The LORD disciplines those he loves.

Proverbs 3:12

Yes, I do.
You need to sit
in the corner
a little longer

You take this
father-child relationship
very seriously

Delight yourself in the LORD and he will give
you the desires of your heart.

Psalm 37:4

Keep getting to know me,
you'll learn more

I didn't understand

Therefore if anyone is in Christ, he is a new creation.
The old things have passed away. Behold,
all things have become new.

2 Corinthians 5:17 (WEB)

You are beautiful, my child.

Before

After

But the fruit of the Spirit is love, joy, peace,
patience, kindness, goodness, faith,
gentleness, and self-control.

Galatians 5:22–23 (WEB)

Me too

I like me better.

Again, therefore, Jesus spoke to them, saying,
"I am the light of the world. He who follows
me will not walk in the darkness,
but will have the light of life."

John 8:12 (WEB)

Give thanks to the LORD, for he is good.

Psalm 136:1

In everything give thanks,
for this is the will of God in
Christ Jesus toward you.

1 Thessalonians 5:18 (WEB)

He heals the broken in heart,
and binds up their wounds.

Psalm 147:3 (WEB)

And
I don't use
Band - Aids

My broken heart
is better than
before !

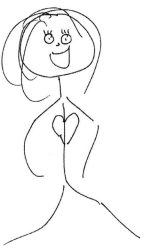